GW00858001

THE ANGEL
BIBLE

THE ANGEL BIBLE
Learning About God's Special Agents
Copyright © 2004 Scandinavia Publishing House
Drejervej 15,3 DK-2400 Copenhagen NV, Denmark
Tel.: (+45) 3531 0330   Fax: (+45) 3531 0334
E-mail: info@scanpublishing.dk
Website: www.scanpublishing.dk
Text copyright © Leyah Jensen
Illustration copyright © Gustavo Mazali
Design by Ben Alex
Printed in China
ISBN 87 7247 790 3 (Hard cover)
ISBN 87 7247 791 1 (Soft cover)

THE ANGEL BIBLE

LEARNING ABOUT GOD'S SPECIAL AGENTS

Text by Leyah Jensen
Illustrations by Gustavo Mazali

scandinavia

Contents

About angels

Angels are servants of God. They are sent from heaven to earth to help people. The angels give messages directly from God himself.

Hebrews 1:14-2:3

Angels at creation

The angels watched as God created the world. Seeing the amazing things he had made, they jumped for joy!

Job 38:7

10

Hagar and her son are rescued

Hagar and her son were lost in the desert. Hagar was sure they were going to die. But God heard the boy crying. Suddenly an angel spoke to Hagar, and told her not to be afraid. God would not let them die. Then her eyes opened, and she saw a well. She picked up her son and gave him a drink. God had rescued them!

Genesis 21:9-21

A wife for Isaac

Abraham and Sarah had a son named Isaac. When Isaac
had grown up, Abraham decided to find him a wife.
Abraham sent his servant out, promising that God would
send an angel to help him find the right woman. Sure
enough, Rebecca came along the road where the servant
stopped and offered him a drink. He asked Rebecca if she
would come back with him and marry Isaac, and she said
yes. The servant thanked God for the angel's help.

Genesis 24:1-67   15

Jacob's dream

Isaac's son Jacob was on a journey
when he stopped to rest for the night.
He laid his head down on a rock and
fell asleep. Then Jacob had a dream.
He saw a stairway from heaven to
earth, with angels going up and down it!
At the top of the stairs stood God. He
told Jacob that He would give him
many descendants, and the land he was
sleeping on. When Jacob woke up, he
praised God for the dream of angels at
heaven's gate.
Genesis 28:10-22

Jacob blesses Joseph's sons

When Jacob was about to die, his son Joseph came to see him. Joseph brought his own sons, Ephraim and Manasseh. Jacob hugged and kissed his grandsons. Then Jacob laid his hands on their heads and said, "May the angel who has saved me from all harm, bless these boys!"
God answered his prayer.
Genesis 48:1-22

19

Moses at the burning bush

Moses was tending his sheep one day when he came to a mountain. There he saw a bush on fire, but it did not burn out. It was the angel of the Lord! When he heard God speak from inside the bush, he was afraid. But God loved Moses, and had a special plan for him. He told him to go and bring the Israelites out of Egypt. Moses did not need to be afraid, because God would be with him.

Exodus 3:1-22

An angel protects the people

Moses freed the Israelites from the cruel Pharaoh, and led them toward the desert. Soon Pharaoh's army came after them. Yet God kept his promise to protect the Israelites—He sent an angel to go behind them. The Israelites escaped, as the angel guarded them from the army.

Exodus 14:1-31

22

The angel leads the people

After the Israelites had escaped the Egyptians, God gave them an angel to go in front and protect them from new enemies. The angel would lead them to the Promised Land that God had prepared for them. God told Moses to listen to the angel, because the angel spoke from God himself. God would bless them as long as they obeyed.

Exodus 23:20-33

A donkey speaks

The King of Moab was afraid of the Israelites, so he sent for Balaam to put a curse on them. The king knew that God was with Balaam. On Balaam's way to see the king, his donkey suddenly stopped in the road. The donkey had seen an angel, blocking the path! Balaam was very angry with the donkey. But then, God made the donkey talk, and Balaam realized that an angel was standing there. Balaam saw that God did not want him to go curse the Israelites.

Numbers 22:21-34

God calls Gideon

An angel came to Gideon and told him that God wanted him to save Israel from its enemies. Gideon did not believe it, because he was the weakest one in his family. He asked the angel for a sign to prove that the

message really came from God. Suddenly, the food in front of Gideon burst into fire. Then Gideon believed! He gathered a small army, and beat their enemies just as the angel had promised he would.

Judges 6:11-24

Samson is born

The Israelites had new enemies called the Philistines. One day, an angel came to an Israelite woman. He told her that she would have a baby that would grow up to save Israel from the Philistines. The woman told her husband, and he came to see the visitor. They didn't realize it was an angel, so they asked him to stay and eat with them. But all of a sudden the food caught fire, and the angel disappeared into the flames.
Then they knew that the visitor was not a man but an angel, and they worshiped God.

Judges 13:1-24

An angel helps Elijah

Elijah was a prophet of God. A bad queen wanted to kill him, so he ran away to the desert. He finally sat down under a tree, so tired that he prayed to die. Then he fell asleep. But soon, an angel came and woke him up. The angel gave Elijah bread to eat and water to drink. When Elijah felt better, the angel sent him along on his journey.

1 Kings 19:1-8

Daniel's friends

An evil king built a statue of gold and ordered everyone to worship it. But Shadrach, Meshach, and Abednego stayed faithful to God and refused to worship the statue. The king threw them into a fiery furnace. But God sent an angel to protect them. When the king looked into the flames, he saw the three men and the angel, unharmed! Then the king knew who the true God was.

Daniel 3:1-30

Daniel in the lions' den

King Darius loved Daniel. The other leaders were jealous, so they planned a trick. They told the king to make everyone worship him. The king agreed. Daniel only worshiped God, so he did not follow the order. The king was forced to throw him into a den of lions. The next day,

the king peeked into the den. Daniel was alive!
He called out, "King, God sent his angel to
shut the lions' mouths!"
Daniel 6:1-28

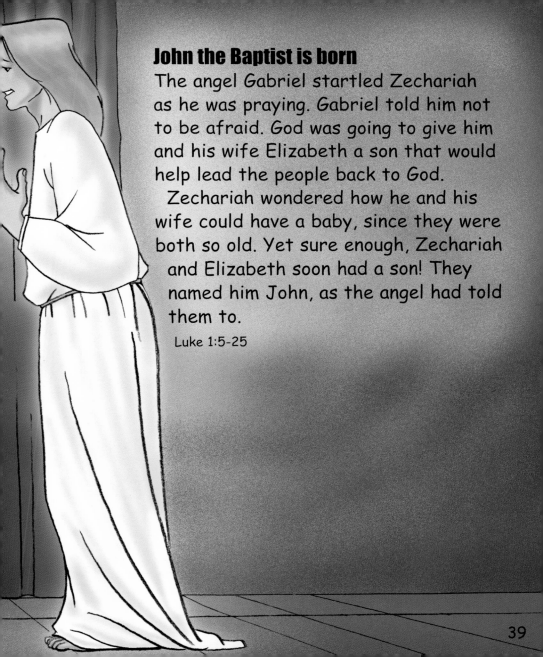

John the Baptist is born

The angel Gabriel startled Zechariah as he was praying. Gabriel told him not to be afraid. God was going to give him and his wife Elizabeth a son that would help lead the people back to God.

Zechariah wondered how he and his wife could have a baby, since they were both so old. Yet sure enough, Zechariah and Elizabeth soon had a son! They named him John, as the angel had told them to.

Luke 1:5-25

Gabriel visits Mary

Mary was faithful to God. She was going
to marry a man named Joseph. One day,
the angel Gabriel visited her. At first
she was afraid, but the angel had a
special message of God's love. God had
chosen her to be the mother of God's
son, Jesus. Mary was very happy, and
praised God for his blessing.

Luke 1:26-38

Jesus is born

Jesus was born in a stable in Bethlehem.
Nearby, shepherds were watching
their sheep at night when an
angel came to them. "Don't be
afraid!" the angel said. "I bring
you good news, that a Saviour
has been born." Suddenly
many more angels appeared.
The shepherds hurried off
  to see Jesus.

Luke 2:8-16

Jesus in the desert

When Jesus had grown up, the Spirit sent him into the desert. He stayed there for forty days. All around him

were wild animals, waiting to snatch him up.
But angels were there to take care of Jesus
and protect him.
Mark 1:12-13

The children's angels

Jesus taught people about heaven, and told them how to live on earth. Jesus loved children very much. God had given them their own special angels! Jesus told people to be kind to children, because their angels were always close to God.

Matthew 18:10-14

47

The angel at the pool

In Jerusalem, there was a pool called Bethesda. Many sick people lay around the pool. Every once in a while, an angel of the Lord came down and stirred up the water. The first person into the moving water would be healed of his sickness.

John 5:2-4

Angels rejoice

Jesus wanted people to know that each of them was precious to God. Jesus said that if just one person turns to God, the angels in heaven would rejoice with gladness!

Luke 15:8-10

The angel at the tomb

After Jesus died, his friend Mary went to visit the tomb where he was laid. Suddenly, there was a loud earthquake! Then an angel came down and rolled away the opening of the tomb. The guards shook with fear. Shining brightly, the angel said to Mary, "Jesus is not here; he has risen!" Mary ran to tell the disciples the good news, as the angel had told her to do.

Matthew 28:1-8

Jesus' friends in prison

People came from all over to hear the apostles teach about Jesus. The church leaders were jealous so they threw the apostles in jail. But then an angel came in the night and let them out. The angel told them to go to the temple and keep teaching.
Acts 5:12-25

Peter in prison

One day, King Herod himself
was angry with the apostles.
He put Peter in jail, and had
him guarded by sixteen soldiers.
Yet God sent help once again.
A light shone in Peter's cell—it
was an angel! The chains fell off
Peter's wrists, and the angel
led him out of the jail. Peter
went to see his friends, and
they all celebrated.
Acts 12:1-19

Angels protect us

The angel of the Lord is with all those who believe in Him. He stays close to care for them.

Psalm 34:7

Angels guard us

If we trust in God, He will command his angels to guard us. They will lift us from all harm. They will give us the power to escape our enemy.
Psalm 91:11-13

Angels visit us

We should love everyone as if they were a part of our own family. We must always be kind to strangers, because they might be angels without our knowing it!

Hebrews 13:1-2